W9-DBV-036

LAKE CLASSICS

*Great Short Stories
from Around the World I*

MORI OGWAI

Stories retold by Joanne Suter
Illustrated by James Balkovek

LAKE EDUCATION
Belmont, California

LAKE CLASSICS

Great American Short Stories I

Washington Irving, Nathaniel Hawthorne, Mark Twain, Bret Harte, Edgar Allan Poe, Kate Chopin, Willa Cather, Sarah Orne Jewett, Sherwood Anderson, Charles W. Chesnutt

Great American Short Stories II

Herman Melville, Stephen Crane, Ambrose Bierce, Jack London, Edith Wharton, Charlotte Perkins Gilman, Frank R. Stockton, Hamlin Garland, O. Henry, Richard Harding Davis

Great British and Irish Short Stories I

Arthur Conan Doyle, Saki (H. H. Munro), Rudyard Kipling, Katherine Mansfield, Thomas Hardy, E. M. Forster, Robert Louis Stevenson, H. G. Wells, John Galsworthy, James Joyce

Great Short Stories from Around the World I

Guy de Maupassant, Anton Chekhov, Leo Tolstoy, Selma Lagerlöf, Alphonse Daudet, Mori Ogwai, Leopoldo Alas, Rabindranath Tagore, Fyodor Dostoevsky, Honoré de Balzac

Cover and Text Designer: Diann Abbott

Library of Congress Catalog Number: 94-075345
ISBN 1-56103-044-9
Printed in the United States of America
1 9 8 7 6 5 4 3 2

CONTENTS

❦ Lake Classic Short Stories ❧

"The universe is made of stories, not atoms."

—Muriel Rukeyser

"The story's about you."

—Horace

Everyone loves a good story. It is hard to think of a friendlier introduction to classic literature. For one thing, short stories are *short*—quick to get into and easy to finish. Of all the literary forms, the short story is the least intimidating and the most approachable.

Great literature is an important part of our human heritage. In the belief that this heritage belongs to everyone, *Lake Classic Short Stories* are adapted for today's readers. Lengthy sentences and paragraphs are shortened. Archaic words are replaced. Modern punctuation and spellings are used. Many of the longer stories are abridged. In all the stories, painstaking care has been taken to preserve the author's unique voice.

Lake Classic Short Stories have something for everyone. The hundreds of stories in the collection cover a broad terrain of themes, story types, and styles. Literary merit was a deciding factor in story selection. But no story was included unless it was as enjoyable as it was instructive. And special priority was given to stories that shine light on the human condition.

Each book in the *Lake Classic Short Stories* is devoted to the work of a single author. Little-known stories of merit are included with famous old favorites. Taken as a whole, the collected authors and stories make up a rich and diverse sampler of the story-teller's art.

Lake Classic Short Stories guarantee a great reading experience. Readers who look for common interests, concerns, and experiences are sure to find them. Readers who bring their own gifts of perception and appreciation to the stories will be doubly rewarded.

❦ Mori Ogwai ❧
(1862–1922)

About the Author

Mori Ogwai was born in Tsuwano, Shimane, Japan, in 1862. As a boy he was interested in science. At the age of 21, he graduated from medical school.

In 1884 he went to Germany as an army doctor. He stayed there for four years, studying the hygiene practices of the German army. During this period he learned the German language and developed an appreciation of German literature. His first novel *Maihime* was based on his experiences there.

Dr. Mori remained an army surgeon until 1916. Yet all through his medical career he continued writing. More than 60 novels and short stories followed the publication of his first book in 1890.

In addition to his own writing, Mori translated numerous German classics into Japanese. He also translated stories by the American authors Washington Irving and Bret Harte.

When it first appeared, "Takase Bune" was praised as "a clear reflection of the Japanese spirit." The simple tale is set in the 18th century, when Japan was under the iron rule of the Shoguns. The two characters, a humble prisoner and a guard, represent centuries of Japanese experience and thought.

"The Pier" presents yet another very interesting example of the Japanese character. In this story, Mori's noble lady shows that social rank has little effect on the moral sentiment of the Japanese people. Critics admired the dignified tone of this story. They compared it to the work of the great French writers Flaubert and Merimee.

In all of his writing, Mori Ogwai wrote in a classical rather than an experimental style. His body of work had a great influence on modern Japanese literature.

Takase Bune

Are the facts the same as the truth? In this touching story, a prisoner tells the truth behind the facts of his crime. Why is his story so different from the police report?

"I HAVE TO TELL YOU A SHAMEFUL THING. I HAVE NEVER
BEFORE HAD AS MUCH AS 200 PENNIES."

Takase Bune

Takase bune is a small river boat. In the Far East such a flat-bottomed boat is called a *junk*. This junk sails up and down the river Takase in Kyoto, Japan.

In the old days, when a person in Kyoto broke a law, that person would be sent away to a distant prison island. Before the criminal was sent off, the members of his family were called out to the jail house. There they were allowed to visit their loved one. Then the criminal and one family member were taken to Takase bune. That night the junk would sail to the sea coast city of Osaka.

The man who took charge of the criminal was a Doshin, or private. He was under the command of Machibugyo, the head judge of the city of Kyoto. It was usual for this private to allow one family member to go on board the junk with the criminal. This was not exactly following the letter of the law. The government pretended not to know about it. This custom was called "looking over with generous eye"—or letting things slip by.

It is a terrible punishment to be sent off to a distant island. The people of Kyoto thought that these criminals must have done great crimes. Most of them, however, had done nothing so terrible as murder or setting fires. Many of the prisoners who went on board Takase bune were not really evil. Many were people who broke the law without really meaning to. Some, in fact, did not completely understand what they had done. One criminal, for example, had tried to kill himself along with his lover. But, by accident, he had remained alive after she died.

After taking such criminals on board, Takase bune was rowed out at the same time each evening. It was just when sunset bells began to ring from the temples. Then the little junk ran toward the east. It silently glided by the dark houses of Kyoto on either shore. Finally it went down and across the river Kamo.

In this junk, the criminals and their family members often talked over their lives. Late into the night they talked. Over and over they said how sorry they were. But it was too late.

The private acted as the guard. He sat beside the criminals and their loved ones. In this way he heard the sad stories of the criminals' lives. The private often heard surprising tales. They were not the stories told in court. There was nothing of these stories in the written statements of the police. The judges who decided the cases could never dream of such stories.

There were different kinds of men who took the job of the private. Some of them were cold-hearted. They were not moved by the unhappy stories. They almost wanted to cover their ears. But some of the other privates were deeply moved by the sorrows of other people. Their hearts were touched. But they took care not to show their feelings while doing their official duty. Sometimes a criminal with an especially sad story happened to be guarded by a private with an especially soft heart. Then, the private could not help weeping.

Therefore, the guarding of Takase bune was a job that no one wanted. The privates all thought it was the very worst job in the city of Kyoto's government.

* * *

When was it? Perhaps it may have been during the age of Kwansei, just before 1800. This was the time when Marquis Shirakawa Rakuwo had ruling power. It was the time when the capital city of Tokyo was still called Edo.

It was a lovely evening in spring. The cherry blossoms around the temple fell gently as the sunset bells rang. A strange criminal was about to go to Takase bune. He was not like any that had ever been seen before.

This prisoner's name was Kisuke. He was a man of about 30 years of age. He had no place to call home. He had no family to visit him at the prison house. Kisuke went on the junk all alone.

Haneda Shobei was the private who had been ordered to guard him. On this beautiful evening, he took the criminal on board Takase bune. His prisoner was a stranger to him, of course. He had heard only that this Kisuke was guilty of the crime of killing his brother. Now, Haneda Shobei looked the man over as he was taking him from the prison house to the pier.

Kisuke was thin and pale. The private found him quite frank and quick to obey. He showed respect for Shobei as an officer of the government. The prisoner Kisuke did not cause trouble in any way. The man seemed truly agreeable. And he did not appear to be putting on an act as many criminals did.

Shobei thought it was strange. After they went on board, he watched Kisuke very closely.

The wind had stopped blowing early that evening. A thin cloud covered the whole face of the sky. The moon was nearly hidden. The coming warmth of summer was felt. It rose like a fog both from the earth on the shore and from the river bed.

Soon Takase bune left the city of Kyoto behind. It passed across the river Kamo, and all became quiet. The only sound was that of the waves. They were gently washing against the side of the boat as it split the water.

All criminals on board Takase bune were allowed to sleep in the boat at night. But Kisuke did not even lie down. He kept silent, looking at the moon. The moonlight changed from bright to dim, as the thickness of the cloud changed. Kisuke's face looked peaceful in the pale light. His forehead did not wrinkle with anger or fear. His eyes were quite bright.

Shobei did not look straight at Kisuke's face. But he watched him closely out of the corner of his eye. In his mind, the private kept repeating, "This is strange. This is strange." It was not the usual thing for a prisoner's face to look so completely happy. But Kisuke looked as if he might begin to whistle or hum a song.

Shobei thought back. He could not remember how many trips he had taken on Takase bune. But all the criminals he had ever seen on the junk had the same miserable look. It was such a sad look that he could hardly bear to see it. Now, what is the matter with this man? He looks as if he is on a picnic boat.

It is said that he killed his brother. It doesn't matter how hateful a man the brother was. It does not matter what brought about the killing. If this man has a human heart, he must be feeling guilty and ashamed.

Shobei stared at the pale, thin fellow. Can he be such an evil man that he is completely without human feeling? He does not seem so. Is he, by chance, a mad man? No, no! His words and actions do not show that he is mad. The more he thought about Kisuke, the harder it became for Shobei to understand him.

Shobei wondered more and more about the man. He spoke to the prisoner at last:

"Kisuke, what are you thinking?"

"Yes, sir," replied Kisuke. He quickly looked around him. He seemed to be afraid he had done something wrong. Now he looked closely at Shobei to see what he had done.

Shobei felt that he must make himself clear. His sudden questions had not come as part of his official duty. Now he thought that he should explain. So he said thus:

"No, I did not mean to ask you questions with any special meaning. In fact, I only wanted to know your feelings about going to the island. I have guarded a great many people in this junk. Though they were men of different lives, all were alike in one way. They were all sorry to be going to the island prison. All of them cried through the night. Every man hung onto the family member who sailed on this junk with him. But looking at you— I think you do not worry about going to the island. What are you thinking of?"

Kisuke smiled. He said:

"I thank you for your kind words. Indeed, it must be a sad thing for other people to go to the island. I can understand their feeling. But that is only because they spent easy lives in the world. No doubt the city of Kyoto is a wonderful place. But there will never again be such misery as I went through there.

"The government was good to me. It saved my life when it ordered me to be sent to the island. However sad that island may be, it cannot be the place where the worst demons live. I never have had a place that I could call my home. But now the government has ordered me to make the island my home. It has allowed me to stay there without worry.

"This is the first thing that I am so thankful for. You see, I have never fallen sick, even though my body looks quite weak. So I think I will not hurt my body by working hard on the island. Also, as I was to be sent to the island, I was given 200 pennies. I have them here."

Saying this, Kisuke placed his hand on his chest. His purse was hanging on a string around his neck. It was the law at that time to give prisoners a small amount of money. A person who was sent off to the island was given 200 pieces of copper.

Kisuke went on: "I have to tell you a

shameful thing. I never have had as much as 200 pennies in my pocket. I tried to get work everywhere. When I got work, I worked very hard. But I had to give all the money I earned into another man's hand.

"I was doing pretty well if I could live from hand to mouth—getting only enough money to buy food. Just when I would pay off what I owed, I would have to borrow again. But then I was put into the prison house. There I was fed without doing any work. I cannot help but feel thankful to the government for this single fact.

"Besides, I was given these 200 pennies! If I can live on the things the government gives me, then I can keep these 200 pennies. I will not have to spend them. This is the first time that I ever had money which need not be spent. I do not know what kind of work I can do on the island. When I land there, I will find out. But I am looking forward happily to saving up these 200 pennies. And I want to learn to do a new kind of work on the island."

After he said this, Kisuke became silent.

Shobei said, "So, is that it?" Then he also became silent for a while. He was lost in deep thought. Everything he had heard was quite different from what he had expected to hear.

Shobei was nearing the beginnings of old age. He already had four children by his wife. Counting his old mother, his family had seven members. He watched his money so closely that he might be called cheap. He would not buy any clothes except those he wore at the office.

Unfortunately, however, his wife came from the family of a rich man. She tried to live upon what Shobei earned. But she could not watch what she spent closely enough to please her husband. She still had the ways of a spoiled child in a rich family.

Quite often they ran out of money at the end of the month. Then his wife would borrow money from her home. She borrowed secretly. She knew that her husband hated owing money as much as a farmer hates caterpillars. But such things are hard to hide from a husband.

Shobei did not like to take anything from her home. Even on such days as the five festivals, he did not want gifts. He did not like the children to take presents of clothing even on their birthdays. He certainly did not like to think that her family had to buy what he could not buy himself. This is the reason why the storms blew, now and then, in the home of Haneda Shobei. It was money alone that broke the peace.

Shobei listened now to the story of Kisuke. He compared the life of Kisuke to his own. Kisuke said that he had to spend every bit of the money he earned just to live. What a sad and miserable life that was!

Then Shobei thought about his own life. Surely he was very different from Kisuke. But wasn't he also one who lived only by taking what the government gave him? Didn't he also have to spend every cent that he got? And he had no savings like the 200 pennies that were so dear to the prisoner Kisuke.

It was not surprising that Kisuke was pleased with the 200 coins. He had never had anything before. But there was even a more wonderful thing—the feeling of satisfaction that Kisuke now had.

Kisuke suffered when he could not find much work in the world. But once he had found it, he worked hard. He was happy to get enough to keep from going hungry. Kisuke was happily surprised when he was taken to the prison house. He found that food—which was so hard to get at that time—was given without any work. It was like a gift from heaven. He felt a peacefulness which he had never known before.

Here, Shobei found a great difference between them. As a private, he had a steady job and could count on his pay. Though he sometimes was short of money, the sums he spent and took in were regular. This was life as he knew it and expected it to be. But he never felt satisfaction from it. Generally he felt that his life was neither good nor bad.

In the deeper part of Shobei's mind, however, a worry was always there. He worried about what he should do if, while living this way, he suddenly fell sick. Or what if he were suddenly let go from his

job? This worry came to his mind
whenever he learned that his wife had
borrowed money from her home.

Why was there this difference between
him and his prisoner? Looking from the
outside, he thought that it was only
because Kisuke had no family counting
on him. He, Shobei, had a family. But
there must be more to it. Even if he were
a single man, Shobei did not think that
he could feel as satisfied as Kisuke. He
thought there must be a deeper reason.

Shobei tried to think about the ways
of human life. When one has an illness,
he thinks that life would be good if only
this illness were gone. When one has no
dinner meal, he thinks all would be well
if he could only eat! When he has no
savings put away, he thinks only of
hiding away a small amount of money.

Yet even then, if he had some money,
a man would wish for a little more!

Thus—from one wish to another—man does not seem to stop, no matter how far he goes. Shobei now thought that this Kisuke had taught him a lesson. He had showed Shobei that he must stop.

Shobei looked at Kisuke with new wonder. It seemed to him now that an angel's halo was somehow shining over the prisoner's head.

Shobei watched Kisuke's face. The young man was looking up to the sky. Then Shobei spoke to him again.

"Kisuke san."

This time he said "san" or "mister"— but he had not changed the name on purpose. As soon as he heard his own voice, Shobei knew that this was not fitting. "Mister" was a title of honor and respect. But he could not take back the word that had already been spoken.

Kisuke replied, "Yes, sir." There was a strange look on his face. He seemed to wonder why his name was called with "san." He looked shyly at Shobei.

Shobei said, "I may be asking too many questions. But I have heard that you are going to the island because you have killed a man. Would you mind telling me the story?"

Kisuke said, "I would be glad to, sir." Then, as if standing before a court, he began to tell his story in a low voice.

"I really have no excuse for myself. I did such a terrible thing. There was a great misunderstanding. Thinking it over later, even I myself cannot quite understand why such a thing happened. Things got carried away.

"I lost my parents to a sickness when I was small. When they died, I was left alone with my younger brother. At first the people in our neighborhood felt sorry for us. They let us do errands and such things for them. This way we grew up without dying of hunger or cold. Even when we grew older and when we looked for work, we helped each other. We tried to stay together and care for each other as long as we could.

"Then came the fall of the last year. My brother and I were working at a weaving factory at Nishijin. We were doing the work of drying the yarn. After a time my brother had fallen sick. He could not work any more.

"At that time we were living in a place that was a sort of a barn. I went to the weaver's by crossing the bridge over the river. In the evening, I always came home with food and other things. My brother was always waiting for me. He felt ashamed that he stayed at home sick. He said that it was wrong to let me work alone.

"One day I came home as usual, without any special worries. There I found my brother lying on the bed with his face down. There was blood all around him. I was shocked. I quickly threw down the packages of food. I rushed to him and cried, 'What is the matter! What is the matter!'

"Then my brother lifted up his face. It was as white as death, and marked with blood from cheeks to chin. He saw me, but he could not speak. Only a hissing sound came out each time he breathed.

"I could not understand this at all. I tried to take a better look. I said, 'What is the matter with you? Did you spit up the blood?' My brother raised up his body a bit. He rested on his right hand on the bed. His left hand was holding tight to a wound under his chin. From that place dark blood was flowing between his fingers.

"My brother's eyes seemed to ask me not to come nearer. He opened his mouth.

At last he was able to speak a few words. 'Forgive me, please,' he said. 'You know I am never going to get well from this sickness. I have decided to hurry my death. That will make things a little easier for you, my brother. I thought I could die if I cut my wind-pipe. But only the breath came out. I tried to push in deeper, deeper, but my hand slipped. It seems that the blade was not broken. I may be able to die if you take this out. It is so hard to speak. Help me, please. Take it out.'

"When my brother loosened his hand, his breath hissed out again from the wound. My own voice was choked. I could not speak. Silently I looked at my brother's throat. It seemed to me that he had cut across his wind-pipe with a razor. When he did not die by that, he had pushed the razor into his throat to cut in deeper. I saw about two inches of the razor's handle. I looked, but did not know what to do. I could only watch the face of my brother. My brother was also watching me.

"'Wait,' I said at last. 'I will run for a doctor.' Then my brother looked into my face with angry eyes. Holding his throat tight with his left hand, he cried, 'What can the doctor do? Oh! It hurts so badly! Quick, take it out! I beg you!'

"I did not know what to do. I was still looking at the face of my brother. It is strange how a man's eyes can speak at such a time. My brother's eyes said to me, 'Do it quick, quick!'

"I felt that the inside of my head was turning around like a wheel. But the eyes of my brother did not stop that awful begging. And the anger in his eyes was growing stronger and stronger. At last they became such fierce eyes as those that look from the face of an enemy.

"Seeing this, I felt that I must do as he asked. I said, 'It cannot be helped. I will take it out.' And at that moment the look in my brother's eyes changed. Now he looked peaceful and happy. I thought I must do the deed in one quick move. First I bent my body forward so that I was kneeling. Then I held the handle of the razor tightly and drew it out.

"Just at that moment I saw the front door opening. An old woman was entering the house. She was the old woman I had hired to take care of my brother while I was away. Each work day she helped him drink his medicine and do other things. Now it was already dark in the house. I do not know how much she had seen. She cried, 'Alas!' Then she ran out, leaving the door open.

"When I pulled out the razor, I took care to pull it quickly and straight. But my hand was shaking. I cut some part of his throat that was not cut before. The blade was facing to the outside. It may have been that a part of his neck on that side was cut.

"With the razor still in my hand, I stared blankly at the old woman coming in and running out. It was after she went away that I seemed to wake up. I looked at my brother. He was already dead. A great deal of blood was pouring from the wound. Thus I sat, looking at him, with the razor beside me. I stared at the face of my brother, dead with half-opened eyes. Then the policemen from the town came and took me to the office."

While Kisuke had told his story, he was looking up into Shobei's face. After he said this last sentence, he dropped his eyes.

The story of Kisuke made sense. Maybe it made too much sense, Shobei thought. Perhaps this was because he had gone over the whole thing so many times. He had a chance to practice his story each time he told it at the city office. And he practiced it again before the court of the government.

Listening to him, Shobei felt as if he was looking at the very scene. But when Kisuke was only halfway through his telling of the story, Shobei had begun to wonder. What was true and what was not? Was this really a case of a brother murdering a brother? He could not answer that question even when he heard all of the story.

The brother had asked him to pull out the razor. The sick man wanted to die. So Kisuke pulled it out, and let him die. This may be called murder. But it seemed to Shobei that the brother would have died even if he had been left alone.

The poor sick man wanted to die sooner because he could not bear the pain. And Kisuke could not bear to see the pain. Hoping to spare his brother pain, he cut short his life. Is this a crime? Surely the fact that one man kills another is a crime. But is it possible to kill someone who is already on the brink of death? He could not answer the question by any means.

Shobei thought and thought about it. Suddenly he very much wanted to put the whole matter into the hands of someone else. He wanted someone who was above him, someone with more power, to decide. He wanted to do whatever that person in power said to do. He wished to make the judgment of the Honorable Judge and the court his own. But even though he wanted this— there was something in his mind that he could not understand. Somehow he wanted to ask the Honorable Judge about it.

The gloomy night passed, hour by hour. Takase bune, carrying its two silent men, sailed along upon the dark water.

Hanako

Is beauty in the eye of the beholder? In this story a famous sculptor interviews a new model. To everyone else the girl looks very plain and ordinary. What does the artist see in her?

THE MAN SAID THAT HE HAD BROUGHT MADEMOISELLE
HANAKO—AS HE HAD PROMISED.

Hanako

The great artist Auguste Rodin came into the studio.

The large room was filled with sunlight. It was the largest room in the Hotel Biron—a fine and beautiful building. Years ago it had been built by a rich man. But later on the building had been used as a convent. Then it was called the School of the Sacred Heart. Until a short time ago, it was the finest girls' school in the town of St. Germain.

Perhaps the nuns of the Sacred Heart taught lessons in this very sunlit room.

Or perhaps they taught the little French girls their songs here. Do not little birds cry out when they see from their nest that their mother is coming near? Just so, the little girls may have stood in rows here. When the nun called out, they may have opened their mouths and sung.

Those happy voices no longer may be heard here.

But another sort of happiness is now present in this room. A different kind of life fills it. This life has no voice. But— though silent—it is wonderful, rich, and very fine.

There were several lumps of gypsum in the room. Big piles of the plaster-like material sat on each of several tables. The master usually begins several works at a time. He will work on one for a while, and then go to another. In just this way he works, according to his mood, until they are finished. As different plants begin to bloom at the same time, so certain of his works grow. Like things in nature, some grow quickly, some slowly.

This man, Auguste Rodin, has a great feel for form and shape. His wonderful works of art are growing in his mind before his hands touch them. He has a great power for deep thought. The moment he begins a work, he is deep into it. He is like a man who has been at work for hours on end.

On this day Rodin's face was bright. He looked over the many half-finished works with a smile. His was a face with a wide forehead and a nose that had a bend in the middle. He wore a white, full beard that crowded about his chin.

There were knocks at the door.

In French he called for the visitor to come in: "Entrez." Auguste Rodin's voice was deep and powerful. His words seemed to cut through the air of the room. His voice did not sound like that of an old man.

The man who entered the door was a thin fellow with brown hair. He was about 30 years of age. Politely, he bowed his head in greeting. Then he said that he had brought Mademoiselle Hanako—as he had promised.

Rodin neither smiled nor frowned when he saw the man entering, and his face did not change at all when he heard what the man said to him.

Once a captain from Cambodia had been staying in Paris. At that time Rodin saw a dancer whom this captain had brought with him from his own country. Rodin noticed the easy movements of her long, slender arms and legs. As he watched her dance, he quickly made some drawings. He has these drawings still. Rodin has certain beliefs about beauty. As in the case of the dancer, he believes that every person has something of beauty.

Now Rodin had heard about a Japanese girl called Hanako. She had been on stage at the theater in that small French town. So he had sent a message to the man who had charge of Hanako. He asked him to bring the actress to his house.

The man who had just come to the door was the actress's manager.

"Let her come in," Rodin said. He did not show the manager to a chair.

"Hanako does not speak French," he said. "I have brought an interpreter with us. He speaks both French and Japanese. He can help you talk with the girl."

"Who is he?" asked Rodin. "Is he a Frenchman?"

"No, a Japanese. He is a student. He heard from Hanako that she was called to visit you. He wanted to come along so he could serve as your interpreter."

"All right. Let him enter also."

In an instant, two Japanese, a man and a woman, entered the room. Both of them looked unusually small. The manager, who followed and closed the door, was not a tall man. But the two Japanese reached only to his ears.

Now Rodin's face wrinkled about the eyes. His eyes always did this when he looked at things closely. The wrinkles seem to be cut into the skin at the inner corner of his eyes. Rodin looked from the student to Hanako. Then he looked at only her for a while. The student bowed slightly. He shook the right hand that Rodin held out. It was a hand on which each vein and muscle stood out under the skin. It was the hand that had created art works that were famous all over the world. *The Bather, The Kiss,* and *The Thinker* were the names of his most beautiful statues. Now the student took out a card on which "Kubota, M.P.," was written. He gave it to Rodin.

Rodin looked quickly at the card. He said:

"Are you studying in France?"

"Yes, sir."

"Have you been here for some time? Do you do good work?"

Kubota was not surprised. He had been told that Rodin always asked this same question. Now, these simple words were spoken directly to him.

"Oui," he nodded, answering yes in French. *"Beaucoup, monsieur!* I do very good work."

At the moment he said this, Kubota felt as if he were promising to work hard for the rest of his life.

Kubota introduced Hanako. Rodin looked down as if to take in all of her with a quick glance of the eye. He saw

Hanako's small, trim body. He saw the stiff, formal hair of the actress. He saw the tips of her feet in their white stockings and sandals. Finally he reached out and took the tiny but firm hand.

Kubota knew that he was in the presence of greatness. It made him feel humble. He wished that he had a finer person to introduce to Rodin as a Japanese woman. His feeling was not completely without reason. Hanako was not a beauty. She was appearing in many European cities as a Japanese actress. But in Japan, she was not at all well-known.

Of course, Kubota also knew nothing about her. Indeed, an actress did not have to be a beauty. It might have been too harsh to call her a servant. Her hands and feet did not show that she had done hard work. She had only reached the tender young age of 17. Yet even in her bloom, she was hardly good-looking enough to work as a chambermaid. In a word, she was not any better to look at than a nursery maid.

But, surprisingly, Rodin's face showed a happy glow. He was pleased with Hanako. She looked healthy. To him, it was clear she had not spent too much time at rest. Her skin was firm and tight from plenty of exercise. This showed clearly in her face which was short from forehead to chin. It showed in the bare wrists and hands. It showed in the thin skin that had not a bit of fat.

Hanako already knew European manners. Now she took the hand of Rodin. He smiled in a friendly way.

Rodin offered chairs to both of them. He said to the manager:

"Please wait for us a while in the next room."

After the manager was gone, they sat down.

Rodin offered the open box of cigars to Kubota. Then he said to Hanako:

"Are there any mountains or sea near Mademoiselle's home?"

Hanako shared a common custom with other young women of the theater. She had a carefully prepared story of her life all ready to tell. Whenever she was questioned, she told this set story and no other. By now she had told the story over and over again many times. It had become like something out of a book. But the unexpected question of Rodin upset this ready-made plan.

"The mountain is at a distance. The sea is close by."

The answer pleased Rodin.

"Did you ride on junks often? I find those little ships of the Far East most colorful and interesting."

"Yes, sir."

"Did you row yourself?"

"No, sir. I did not row. I was still very small when I lived at home. My father rowed."

Suddenly a picture came into Rodin's imagination. He became silent for a while. The great artist is a man who is often silent.

Then Rodin turned to Kubota. He spoke softly to the young man. "I suppose that Mademoiselle knows my work. Would she be willing to take off her clothing?"

Kubota thought for a moment. Of course he did not wish to bring shame to a woman of his own country. Was it proper to ask her to bare herself before a man? But he did not object to putting forth the idea for Rodin. He waited for a moment before he spoke. He was not sure of what Hanako would say in answer.

"Anyway, I will speak to her," Kubota said.

"If you please."

Kubota addressed Hanako in this manner:

"The master has something to ask you about. I think you understand that he is a great sculptor. He is an artist like no other in the world. He models the shape of the human body. This is the point about which he wishes to speak with you.

"He wishes to know if you will help him. He would like you to sit for him in the nude for a few moments. What do you say? As you see, he is an elderly man—not very far from 70. And everyone knows that he is a fine gentleman. What do you think?"

Thus saying, Kubota looked closely into Hanako's face. He was wondering whether she would turn away in shame. Would she act as if she were shocked? Or would she be angry with him?

"I will," she replied openly, like a child.

"She says she will," Kubota told Rodin.

Rodin's face was bright with pleasure. Getting up from the chair, he took out paper and chalk. He said to Kubota as he laid them on the table:

"Will you stay here?"

"You may need me to help you talk to each other," said Kubota. "But it might be unpleasant to Mademoiselle."

"Then, will you wait there in the library? I should be able to finish my drawing within 15 or 20 minutes. Light a cigar, if you like."

"He says that he will be finished drawing within 15 or 20 minutes." Saying these words to Hanako, Kubota went out through the door shown him.

The small room into which Kubota stepped had doors on either side and only one window. Many books were on the wall across from the window. They lined the other walls, too.

For a while, Kubota stood reading the titles on the leather covers of the books. He saw they were on all different subjects. By nature, Rodin was a book lover. It is said that he was always carrying a book in his hand. This was his habit even in his young days. At that time he had been a poor artist walking the streets of Brussels. In this room, Kubota felt the presence of Rodin, the book-lover. He thought that, among these old dusty books, there must be many memories.

The ashes of his cigar were about to fall. Kubota walked toward the table. He dropped the ashes into the ash tray.

He wondered about the books on the table. These must be books that Rodin was reading now. He walked closer to see them more clearly.

He saw a book on the farthest edge of the table, leaning against the window. At first Kubota thought it was the Bible.

When he opened it, however, he found that it was the works of the French writer Baudelaire.

Without any idea of reading it, he turned to the first page. He saw the title, "The Metaphysics of the Toy." Wondering what was in the book, he all at once began to read it.

The words on the page told about a memory. Baudelaire was writing about a time when he was a little boy. He had been taken to a certain house that had a room full of toys. There he was told he might have his choice.

Baudelaire wrote on about what happens after a child has played with a toy for a while. Something comes over him. He decides to break it. He wonders what there is beyond the thing. If it is a moving toy, he wishes to find out just what makes it move.

In this way, the child begins to wonder about metaphysics—the thoughts and ideas *behind* the things in this world. His mind moves from the physical to the metaphysical, from science to metaphysics. He stops asking *what* a thing is and goes on to ask *why* it is.

The article was only four or five pages long. Kubota, becoming interested, read straight through to the end.

Then there was a knock. The door opened, and Rodin's white-bearded face appeared.

"Pardon me. You must be tired of waiting."

"No, sir, I was reading Baudelaire."

Saying this, Kubota entered the studio. Hanako had already gotten dressed. Two sketches were lying on the table.

"What article of Baudelaire's were you reading?"

"'The Metaphysics of the Toy.'"

"The same idea applies to the human body," Rodin said, smiling. "Form is not interesting simply because it is a form. It is the mirror of the soul. In just that way, the form of the body reflects what is inside the person. The inner flame, showing through the form—that is what is interesting!"

Then Kubota looked shyly at the sketches Rodin had made of Hanako.

"They must be hard to understand," Rodin said. "They are so rough."

After a moment, the great artist went on. "Mademoiselle has a very beautiful body. She has not a bit of fat. Each muscle rises under the skin like the muscle of a fox terrier. The muscles are tight and thick. The size of the joints is made the same as the size of the arms and legs. They are so firm.

"Mademoiselle Hanako could stand on one leg while the other is stretched straight out. Then she is like a tree that has its roots deep in the earth. This is different from the Mediterranean type of body with wide shoulders and hips. It is different, too, from the North European type of body with wide hips but narrow shoulders. It is the beauty of strength."

The Pier

Is it hard to say good-bye
to someone you love? A
Japanese nobleman is about
to leave on a long voyage.
How does his devoted wife
feel about their parting?

DURING THE LONG TRIP OF HER HUSBAND, THIS IS THE
ROOM WHERE HER DREAMS MUST COME AND GO.

The Pier

The pier is long . . . long. . . .

The rails of four railroads cut straight
across the iron bridge. Many long and
short cross-beams connect the rails. They
look like the bars of a xylophone on which
children play tinkling music with small
wood hammers. The cracks between the
cross-beams can be dangerous. People
who walk across the bridge sometimes
catch the heels of their shoes in these
cracks. Now the black waves show
through the cracks here and there.
Sometimes the waves reflect the white

flashes of sunshine on the water.

Today the sky has cleared into a deep blue. On the inside of a train, a woman sits with her husband. She is seeing him off today. Warm inside the train, she remembers that the wind is blowing outside.

When leaving the station of Yokohama, she rides in a rickshaw. A man pulls the two-wheeled cart quickly through the streets of the busy port city. He darts in and out of the Yokohama traffic. Finally she stands on the pier of Tokyo Bay. She finds that the wind is still blowing as if to bite the skin. It flutters the skirts of her long coat.

She wears her long, silver-gray coat loosely on her body. Under it she carries the child of her husband. Her husband is starting off on a trip today, the fifth of March. This day is surely not long before the birth of his child.

Around her shoulders she wears a long scarf made of feathers. They are the feathers of a white ostrich. Holding a light green umbrella with gold tassels, she walks along. She is circled by four of her maids.

The pier is long...long....

Several big ships are tied up on the right and the left of the pier. Some are painted black. Some are painted white.

All lined up together, the big ships are making a fence for the wind. But every time she leaves the place where there are ships, a gust of wind blows. It flutters the skirts of her long, silver-gray coat.

Two years ago her husband had married her. It was just after he had graduated from the university, where he had studied literature. Her husband was a nobleman with the title "count." Just a year ago she had given birth to their first child. It was a daughter, a tiny princess like a jewel. At the end of that year, her husband was named Master of Ceremonies at the Royal Court. And now, he is starting to London. He is going there on official royal business.

Today her husband wears a newly made gray overcoat. He twirls a cane with a crooked handle. He is walking quickly along the pier. The viscount, who has a lower office, is traveling with him. The viscount is taller by a head than the woman's husband. He walks quickly beside him, wearing a traveling suit of the same gray color.

A French ship is tied at the far end of the right side of the pier. This is the ship on which her husband is about to sail across the sea to London.

A stool has been placed on the pier. It is very much like the stool that is used to repair the wires of a trolley. From this stool a gangplank is laid to reach the deck of the ship.

While walking slowly, the woman sees her husband and his fellow traveler, the viscount. The two men are crossing the gangplank and entering the ship.

The group of people looking after them are standing, here and there, on the pier. Almost all of them have come to say good-bye to the woman's husband and the viscount. Perhaps no others on this ship which is about to sail are so important. Perhaps no others are looked at by so many people.

Some of the other passengers are walking toward the stool on which the gangplank is laid. They stop there to wait for their friends. Some of them are standing at another place. This place is a bit before the stool. The blocks and ropes are laid down there.

The woman looks at these people. Among them there must be some who are well-known to her husband. There must also be some who know him only a little.

Somehow, standing under this clear sky, they all seem to be unhappy. Or is that only her fancy?

The pier is long . . . long. . . .

She follows slowly after them. Without knowing it, she looks off to her right. She notices that there are many round windows on the side of the ship. In one of those round windows, she sees the faces and chests of women. Three of these women are between 30 and 40 years of age. They all wear white aprons on their chests. They must be workers on the ship. Perhaps they are the waitresses who serve the passengers of the ship on which her husband is about to sail. Suddenly she feels jealous of even those working women.

There is also a woman on the deck of the ship. She is looking down on the pier. This woman wears a big hat made of white cloth and carries a small leather bag in her hand. Two big eyes, as if painted with shadows, are shining on her wrinkled face. She has a large nose, like a hook. She must be a traveler who is also going on this ship. The woman on the pier is also jealous of her.

The pier is long . . . long. . . .

At last she arrives at the foot of the gangplank. As she walks across, she carefully carries her body, remembering that the second baby of her husband is under the silver-gray coat. Then she carefully steps upon the deck of the big, black-painted ship. She hands the light green umbrella to a maid.

The woman is led by the people who have already come on board. They, too, have come to say good-bye. She walks back along the deck toward the front of the ship. There are rooms for passengers at the end of the way. The room numbers go up from 27 to 39.

The viscount is standing at the door of a room. He speaks to her.

"This is the room, madam."

Peeking into the room, she sees two beds. Under them familiar packages and trunks have been placed. Her husband is standing before one of the beds.

"Look it through, madam. It is like this."

This is the room. She must look through it carefully. During the long, long trip of her husband, this is the room where her dreams must come and go.

A man who seems to be the captain comes in. He speaks to her husband in French. Then he guides him to the dining room of the ship. She follows her husband and the viscount and enters the dining room.

This is a large and beautiful dining room. Each table bears a large flower basket. Soon the people who came to say good-bye are all gathered there.

By the order of this man who looks like the captain, a waiter brings forth many cups. She sees that they are made in the shape of large flowers. The waiter pours champagne into the cups. He passes them among the people. Another waiter brings cakes piled high on a plate. He passes these among the people, too.

Then the people with their cups walk ahead. One after another they stand before her husband and the viscount. Each visitor wishes them a happy trip. They all drink from the cups.

She sits on a small chair beside the table. She is waiting for the time when the good wishes are at an end. Now and then, during his busy moments, her husband lifts his eyes to her.

However, there is no more to be said to her before many people. Also, there is no more to be said to him, before many people.

The bell rings. The people have all said

good-bye to her husband and to the viscount. Now they are going out, one after another. She also goes out of the room, nodding to her husband and to the viscount.

Again crossing the slippery gangplank, she goes down to the pier. She takes the light green umbrella from the hand of her maid. She raises it.

Her husband and the viscount are standing on the deck. They are looking in her direction. She is looking up at them from under her umbrella. She feels that her eyes, as she looks up, are slowly growing larger and larger.

Again the bell rings. A few French sailors begin to untie the rope that anchors the boat. A Japanese worker is standing on the stool at the end of the gangplank. He is preparing to draw down the gangplank. He pulls the rope of the wheel. The gangplank at last leaves the deck.

The noon gun of the city of Yokohama sounds. With this as a signal, the ship silently begins to move.

Two older Europeans are standing on the deck. They seem to be a married couple. They are calling out to an old white-haired man who is standing on the pier. They laugh as if whatever they are saying is very jolly. The white-haired man stands with one of his feet placed on something that is used to roll the ropes. The thing looks like a big spool of thread. The woman thinks that none of these people seem to be unhappy about their parting.

It looks as if the ship is moving. It looks as if the pier is moving. There seems to be a great distance between the place where her husband and the viscount are standing and the place where she is standing. She feels her eyes growing larger and larger.

Some of the people who are looking

after them are running to the end of the pier. She cannot do something so bold. Then suddenly, something white waves from the deck. It is a handkerchief. The woman who wears a big hat of white cloth is holding the handkerchief in her hand. A tall man stands at the end of the pier. He wears a red jacket and tan shoes. A white handkerchief waves also from the hand of this man. This, too, must be a parting in human life.

These two persons set the tone. Soon many handkerchiefs are waved from here and there. White things are waving also from the people who are looking after the count. They are circled in a group around him. Now she grasps the fine white handkerchief which she has brought in her sleeve. But she cannot bring herself to do such a bold thing.

When the ship leaves the pier, it turns a bit to the right. The place where her husband and the viscount were standing has disappeared at last.

Still she can see a boy of about 15 or 16 years of age. He is standing at the back of the ship. The boy wears a thin, blue shirt. He looks cold. What mother is waiting for him in France? Or has he no parents? What is he looking at, standing there by the rail?

Slowly she turns her feet and walks among her maids, who circle her.

The pier is long . . . long. . . .

She looks at the place where the black-painted ship was docked until a short time ago. Now the water is sparkling there. It glitters like the scales of fish, as the small waves reflect the pale sunshine.

Thinking About
the Stories

Takase Bune

1. Where does this story take place? Is there anything unusual about it? What effect does the place have on the characters?

2. Compare and contrast at least two characters in this story. In what ways are they alike? In what ways are they different?

3. Does the main character in this story have an internal conflict? Does a terrible decision have to be made? Explain the character's choices.

Hanako

1. Who is the main character in this story? Who are one or two of the minor characters? Describe each of these characters in one or two sentences.

2. The plot is the series of events that takes place in a story. Usually, story events are linked in some way. Can you name an event in this story that was the cause of a later event?

3. Suppose that this story was the first chapter in a book of many chapters. What would happen next?

The Pier

1. Look back at the illustration that introduces this story. What character or characters are pictured? What is happening in the scene? What clues does the picture give you about the time and place of the story?

2. Some stories are packed with action. In other stories, the key events take place in the minds of the characters. Is this story told more through the characters' thoughts and feelings? Or is it told more through their outward actions?

3. Suppose this story had a completely different outcome. Can you think of another effective ending for this story?

Thinking About
the Book

1. Choose your favorite illustration in this book. Use this picture as a springboard to write a new story. Give the characters different names. Begin your story with something they are saying or thinking.

2. Compare the stories in this book. Which was the most interesting? Why? In what ways were they alike? In what ways different?

3. Good writers usually write about what they know best. If you wrote a story, what kind of characters would you create? What would be the setting?